ESSENTIAL

Asian

p

Contents

Introduction

The Asian continent encompasses a vast geographic area with huge and diverse populations. Among these peoples different religions, customs and histories are found; because of this and the influence of their local resources — whether it be a strong fishing industry or traditional rice growing — they have developed distinct cuisines. This culinary wealth has been combined in *Essential Asian*; bringing together a gastronomic variety of dishes from all over Asia, from Japan to Thailand, and from India to China.

All of the spicy and exotic flavours of Asian cuisine have been combined in this book to suit all palates and diets. The vastness of the continent ensures that you will find recipes for the meat-eater and the vegetarian alike. Meat dishes alone can be found in differing forms, including soups and curries – both of which are important dishes in the Asian world. Although the soup is often served as a starter in the West, in the Orient it is often eaten part way through a main meal to clear the palate. The curry, however, is now a particularly well-accepted and eaten dish in the Occident, partly due to the large Indian populations living in countries such as Great Britain. Yet with nearly 900 million people living in India alone, it is not surprising that this dish can be served in a variety of forms.

Traditional Asian cooking methods have been imported to the West along with its gastronomy. The stir-fry method is now a popular way of cooking in many occidental homes as it is quick and healthy. The wok is the principal instrument used and is essential to many Asian dishes. Across the Far East woks are used in various guises. In India, a large pan or *karahi* is used which sits over a hole in a brick or earth oven. This wok-like vessel is used for braising or frying, curries or *karahi* derive its name from the pan. In Indonesia a *wajan* or wok is used over wood or charcoal for curries, rice dishes and quick stir-fries – the same applies in Japan, Thailand, Singapore and Malaysia. This method of cooking allows the food to be easily combined and tossed due to the pan's high sides. For those who like to enjoy a healthy, balanced diet the wok is perfect as it cooks vegetables very quickly. This helps to retain nutrients and crispness, producing both colourful and flavourful recipes.

The dishes included in this book range from hot and spicy to delicate flavours using fish and vegetables. All of the recipes should be cooked using fresh, crisp vegetables and preferably retain their 'bite'. All of the ingredients are now found in western supermarkets, but more traditional options have been suggested where appropriate. It is worth taking a trip to an Asian supermarket or specialist food shop for high-quality soy sauce and oils.

Spicy Thai Soup with Prawns (Shrimp)

Serves 4

INGREDIENTS

2 tbsp tamarind paste

4 red Thai chilies, very finely chopped

2 cloves garlic, crushed

2.5 cm/1 inch piece Thai ginger, peeled and very finely chopped

4 tbsp fish sauce

2 tbsp palm sugar or caster (superfine) sugar

8 lime leaves, roughly torn

1.2 litres/2 pints/5 cups fish stock

100 g/3½ oz carrots, very thinly sliced

350 g/12 oz sweet potato, diced

100 g/3½ oz/1 cup baby corn

cobs, halved

3 tbsp fresh coriander (cilantro), roughly chopped

100g/3½ oz cherry tomatoes, halved

225 g/8 oz fan-tail prawns (shrimp)

1 Place the tamarind paste, chillies, garlic, ginger, fish sauce, sugar, lime leaves and stock in a large preheated wok. Bring to the boil, stirring constantly.

2 Reduce the heat and add the carrot, sweet potato and baby corn to the mixture in the wok.

3 Leave the soup to simmer, uncovered, for about 10 minutes, or until the vegetables are just tender.

4 Stir the coriander, cherry tomatoes and prawns (shrimp) into the soup and heat through for 5 minutes.

5 Transfer the soup to warm serving bowls and serve hot.

COOK'S TIP

Baby corn cobs have a sweet fragrance and flavour. They are available both fresh and canned.

COOK'S TIP

Thai ginger or galangal is a member of the ginger family, but it is yellow in colour with pink sprouts. The flavour is aromatic and less pungent than ginger.

Coconut & Crab Soup

Serves 4

INGREDIENTS

1 tbsp groundnut oil
2 tbsp Thai red curry paste
1 red (bell) pepper, deseeded and sliced
600 ml/1 pint/2½ cups coconut milk

600 ml/1 pint/2½ cups fish stock
2 tbsp fish sauce
225 g/8 oz canned or fresh white crab meat
225 g/8 oz fresh or frozen crab claws

2 tbsp chopped fresh coriander (cilantro)
3 spring onions (scallions), trimmed and sliced

1 Heat the oil in a large preheated wok.

2 Add the red curry paste and red (bell) pepper to the wok and stir-fry for 1 minute.

3 Add the coconut milk, fish stock and fish sauce to the wok and bring to the boil.

4 Add the crab meat, crab claws, coriander (cilantro) and spring onions (scallions) to the wok. Stir the mixture well and heat thoroughly for 2–3 minutes.

5 Transfer the soup to warm bowls and serve hot.

COOK'S TIP

Coconut milk adds a sweet and creamy flavour to the dish. It is available in powdered form or in tins ready to use.

COOK'S TIP

Clean the wok after each use by washing it with water, using a mild detergent if necessary, and a soft cloth or brush. Do not scrub or use any abrasive cleaner as this will scratch the surface. Dry thoroughly with paper towels or over a low heat, then wipe the surface all over with a little oil. This forms a sealing layer to protect the surface of the wok from moisture and prevents it rusting.

Clear Chicken & Egg Soup

Serves 4

INGREDIENTS

1 tsp salt	1 leek, sliced	1 tbsp dry sherry
1 tbsp rice wine vinegar	125 g/4½ oz broccoli florets	dash of chilli sauce
4 eggs	125 g/4½ oz/1 cup shredded	chilli powder, to garnish
850 ml/1½ pints/3¾ cups	cooked chicken	
chicken stock	2 open-cap mushrooms, sliced	

1 Bring a large saucepan of water to the boil and add the salt and rice wine vinegar. Reduce the heat so that it is just simmering and carefully break the eggs into the water, one at a time. Poach the eggs for 1 minute. Remove the poached eggs with a slotted spoon and set aside.

2 Bring the stock to the boil in a separate pan and add the leek, broccoli, chicken, mushrooms and sherry and season with chilli sauce to taste. Cook for 10–15 minutes.

3 Add the poached eggs to the soup and cook for a further 2 minutes. Carefully transfer the soup and poached eggs to 4 individual soup bowls. Dust with a little chilli powder to garnish and serve immediately.

COOK'S TIP

You could use 4 dried Chinese mushrooms, rehydrated according to the packet instructions, instead of the open-cap mushrooms, if you prefer.

VARIATION

You could substitute 125 g/4½ oz fresh or canned crabmeat or the same quantity of fresh or frozen cooked prawns (shrimp) for the chicken, if desired.

Hot & Sour Soup

Serves 4

INGREDIENTS

2 tbsp cornflour (cornstarch)
4 tbsp water
2 tbsp light soy sauce
3 tbsp rice wine vinegar
$\frac{1}{2}$ tsp ground black pepper
1 small fresh red chilli,
    finely chopped

1 egg
2 tbsp vegetable oil
1 onion, chopped
850 ml/1$\frac{1}{2}$ pints/3$\frac{3}{4}$ cups
    chicken or beef consommé
1 open-cap mushroom, sliced

50 g/1$\frac{3}{4}$ oz skinless chicken
    breast, cut into very thin
    strips
1 tsp sesame oil

1 Blend the cornflour (cornstarch) with the water to form a smooth paste. Add the soy sauce, rice wine vinegar, pepper and chilli and mix together.

2 Break the egg into a separate bowl and beat well.

3 Heat the oil in a preheated wok and fry the onion for 1–2 minutes.

4 Stir in the consommé, mushroom and chicken and bring to the boil. Cook for 15 minutes or until the chicken is tender.

5 Pour the cornflour (cornstarch) mixture into the soup and cook, stirring, until it thickens.

6 As you are stirring, gradually drizzle the egg into the soup, to create threads of egg.

7 Sprinkle with the sesame oil and serve immediately.

COOK'S TIP

Make sure that the egg is poured in very slowly and that you stir continuously to create threads of egg and not large pieces.

Beef & Vegetable Noodle Soup

Serves 4

INGREDIENTS

225 g/8 oz lean beef
1 garlic clove, crushed
2 spring onions (scallions), chopped
3 tbsp soy sauce

1 tsp sesame oil
225 g/8 oz egg noodles
850 ml/1½ pints/3¾ cups beef stock
3 baby corn cobs, sliced

½ leek, shredded
125 g/4½ oz broccoli, cut into florets (flowerets)
pinch of chilli powder

1 Using a sharp knife, cut the beef into thin strips and place them in a shallow glass bowl.

2 Add the garlic, spring onions (scallions), soy sauce and sesame oil and mix together well, turning the beef to coat. Cover and leave to marinate in the refrigerator for 30 minutes.

3 Cook the noodles in a saucepan of boiling water for 3–4 minutes. Drain the noodles thoroughly and set aside until required.

4 Put the beef stock in a large saucepan and bring to the boil.

5 Add the beef, together with the marinade, the baby corn, leek and broccoli. Cover and leave to simmer over a low heat for 7–10 minutes, or until the beef and vegetables are tender and cooked through.

6 Stir in the noodles and chilli powder and cook for a further 2–3 minutes. Transfer to bowls and serve immediately.

COOK'S TIP

Vary the vegetables used, or use those to hand. If preferred, use a few drops of chilli sauce instead of chilli powder, but remember it is very hot!

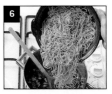

Fish Soup with Wontons

Serves 4

INGREDIENTS
---

125 g/4¹/₂ oz large, cooked,
  peeled prawns (shrimp)
1 tsp chopped chives
1 small garlic clove, finely
  chopped
1 tbsp vegetable oil

12 wonton wrappers
1 small egg, beaten
850 ml/1¹/₂ pints/3³/₄ cups fish
  stock
175 g/6 oz white fish fillet,
  diced

dash of chilli sauce
sliced fresh red chilli and
  chives, to garnish

1 Roughly chop a quarter of the prawns (shrimp) and mix together with the chopped chives and garlic.

2 Heat the oil in a preheated wok and stir-fry the prawn (shrimp) mixture for 1–2 minutes. Remove from the heat and set aside to cool completely.

3 Spread out the wonton wrappers on a work surface (counter). Spoon a little of the prawn (shrimp) filling into the centre of each wonton wrapper. Brush the edges of the wonton wrappers with beaten egg and press the edges together, scrunching them to form a 'moneybag' shape. Set aside while you are preparing the soup.

4 Pour the fish stock into a large saucepan and bring to the boil. Add the diced white fish and the remaining prawns (shrimp) and cook for 5 minutes.

5 Season to taste with the chilli sauce. Add the wontons and cook for a further 5 minutes. Spoon into warmed serving bowls, garnish with sliced red chilli and chives and serve immediately.

VARIATION

Replace the prawns (shrimp) with cooked crabmeat for an alternative flavour.

Spicy Aubergines (Eggplants)

Serves 4

INGREDIENTS

450 g/1 lb aubergines
(eggplants), rinsed
2 tsp salt
3 tbsp vegetable oil
2 garlic cloves, crushed
1 onion, halved and sliced

2.5-cm/1-inch piece fresh root
ginger, chopped
1 fresh red chilli, sliced
2 tbsp dark soy sauce
1 tbsp hoisin sauce
¹/₂ tsp chilli sauce

1 tbsp dark brown sugar
1 tbsp wine vinegar
1 tsp ground Szechuan pepper
300 ml/¹/₂ pint/1 ¹/₄ cups
vegetable stock

1 Cut the aubergines
(eggplants) into cubes
if you are using the larger
variety, or cut the smaller
type in half. Place the
aubergines (eggplants) in a
colander and sprinkle with
the salt. Let stand for
30 minutes. Rinse the
aubergines (eggplants)
under cold running water
and pat dry with kitchen
paper (paper towels).

2 Heat the oil in a
preheated wok and add
the garlic, onion, ginger,
and fresh chilli. Stir-fry for

30 seconds and add the
aubergines (eggplants).
Continue to cook for
1–2 minutes.

3 Add the soy sauce,
hoisin sauce, chilli
sauce, sugar, wine vinegar,
Szechuan pepper and
vegetable stock to the wok,
reduce the heat and leave
to simmer, uncovered, for
10 minutes, or until the
aubergines (eggplants) are
cooked. Increase the heat
and boil to reduce the sauce
until thickened enough to
coat the aubergines

(eggplants). Serve
immediately.

COOK'S TIP

*Sprinkling the aubergines
(eggplants) with salt and
letting them stand removes
the bitter juices, which
would otherwise taint the
flavour of the dish.*

Spring Rolls

Serves 4

INGREDIENTS

175 g/6 oz cooked pork, chopped

75 g/2³/₄ oz cooked chicken, chopped

1 tsp light soy sauce

1 tsp light brown sugar

1 tsp sesame oil

1 tsp vegetable oil

225 g/8 oz beansprouts

25 g/1 oz canned bamboo shoots, drained, rinsed and chopped

1 green (bell) pepper, seeded and chopped

2 spring onions (scallions), sliced

1 tsp cornflour (cornstarch)

2 tsp water

vegetable oil, for deep-frying

SKINS:

125 g/4¹/₂ oz/1¹/₈ cups plain (all-purpose) flour

5 tbsp cornflour (cornstarch)

450 ml/16 fl oz/2 cups water

3 tbsp vegetable oil

1 Mix the pork, chicken, soy, sugar and sesame oil. Cover and marinate for 30 minutes. Heat the vegetable oil in a wok. Add the beansprouts, bamboo shoots, (bell) pepper and spring onions (scallions) and stir-fry for 2–3 minutes. Add the meat and the marinade to the wok and stir-fry for 2–3 minutes. Blend the cornflour (cornstarch) with the water and stir the mixture into the wok. Cool.

2 To make the skins, mix the flour and cornflour (cornstarch) and gradually stir in the water, to make a smooth batter. Heat a small, oiled frying pan (skillet). Swirl one-eighth of the batter over the base and cook for 2–3 minutes. Repeat with the remaining batter. Cover with a damp tea towel (dish cloth).

3 Spread out the skins and spoon one-eighth

of the filling along the centre of each. Brush the edges with water and fold in the sides, then roll up.

4 Heat the oil for deep-frying in a wok to 180°C/350°F. Cook the spring rolls, in batches, for 2–3 minutes, or until golden and crisp. Remove from the oil with a slotted spoon and drain on absorbent kitchen paper (paper towels). Serve.

Sweet & Sour Battered Prawns (Shrimp)

Serves 4

INGREDIENTS

---

16 large raw prawns (shrimp),
    peeled
1 tsp grated fresh root ginger
1 garlic clove, crushed
2 spring onions (scallions),
    sliced
2 tbsp dry sherry
2 tsp sesame oil
1 tbsp light soy sauce
vegetable oil, for deep-frying

shredded spring onion
    (scallion), to garnish

BATTER:
4 egg whites
4 tbsp cornflour (cornstarch)
2 tbsp plain (all-purpose) flour

SAUCE:
2 tbsp tomato purée
    (tomato paste)

3 tbsp white wine vinegar
4 tsp light soy sauce
2 tbsp lemon juice
3 tbsp light brown sugar
1 green (bell) pepper, seeded
    and cut into thin
    matchsticks
$^{1}/_{2}$ tsp chilli sauce
300 ml/$^{1}/_{2}$ pint/$1^{1}/_{4}$ cups
    vegetable stock
2 tsp cornflour (cornstarch)

---

1 Using tweezers, devein the prawns (shrimp), then flatten them with a knife.

2 Place the prawns (shrimp) in a dish and add the ginger, garlic, spring onions (scallions), sherry, oil and soy. Cover and marinate for 30 minutes.

3 Make the batter by beating the egg whites until thick. Fold in the cornflour (cornstarch) and flour to form a light batter.

4 Place all of the sauce ingredients in a pan and bring to the boil. Reduce the heat and leave to simmer for 10 minutes.

5 Remove the prawns (shrimp) from the marinade and dip them into the batter to coat.

6 Heat the oil until almost smoking. Reduce the heat and fry the prawns (shrimp) for 3–4 minutes, until crisp. Serve with the sauce.

Chilli Beef Stir-Fry Salad

Serves 4

INGREDIENTS
---

450 g/1 lb lean rump steak
2 cloves garlic, crushed
1 tsp chilli powder
¹/₂ tsp salt
1 tsp ground coriander

1 ripe avocado
30 ml/2 tbsp sunflower oil
425 g/15 oz can red kidney beans,
    drained
175 g/6 oz cherry tomatoes,
    halved

1 large packet tortilla chips
shredded iceberg lettuce
chopped fresh coriander (cilantro),
    to serve

---

1 Using a sharp knife, slice the beef into thin strips.

2 Place the garlic, chilli powder, salt and ground coriander in a large bowl and mix until well combined.

3 Add the strips of beef to the marinade and toss well to coat all over.

4 Using a sharp knife, peel the avocado. Slice the avocado lengthways and then crossways to form small dice.

5 Heat the oil in a large preheated wok. Add the beef and stir-fry for 5 minutes, tossing frequently.

6 Add the kidney beans, tomatoes and avocado and heat through for 2 minutes.

7 Arrange a bed of tortilla chips and iceberg lettuce around the edge of a large serving plate and spoon the beef mixture into the centre. Alternatively, serve the tortilla chips and iceberg lettuce separately.

8 Garnish with chopped fresh coriander (cilantro) and serve immediately.

COOK'S TIP

Serve this dish immediately as avocado tends to discolour quickly. Once you have cut the avocado into dice, sprinkle it with a little lemon juice to prevent discoloration.

Seven Spice Aubergines (Eggplant)

Serves 4

INGREDIENTS

450 g/1 lb aubergines (eggplants), wiped	50 g/1³/₄ oz/3¹/₂ tbsp cornflour (cornstarch)	1 tbsp Thai seven spice seasoning oil, for deep-frying
1 egg white	1 tsp salt	

1 Using a sharp knife, slice the aubergines (eggplants) into thin rings.

2 Place the egg white in a small bowl and whip until light and foamy.

3 Mix together the cornflour, salt and seven spice powder on a large plate.

4 Heat the oil for deep-frying in a large wok.

5 Dip each piece of aubergine (eggplant) into the beaten egg white then coat in the cornflour and seven spice mixture.

6 Deep-fry the coated aubergine (eggplant) slices, in batches, for 5 minutes, or until pale golden and crispy.

7 Transfer the aubergines (eggplants) to absorbent kitchen paper and leave to drain. Transfer to serving plates and serve hot.

COOK'S TIP

Thai seven spice seasoning can be found in the spice racks of most large supermarkets.

COOK'S TIP

The best oil to use for deep-frying is groundnut oil which has a high smoke point and mild flavour, so it will neither burn or taint the food. About 600 ml/1 pint oil is sufficient.

Mullet with Ginger

Serves 4

INGREDIENTS

1 whole mullet, cleaned and
scaled
2 spring onions (scallions),
chopped
1 tsp grated fresh root ginger
125 ml/4 fl oz/½ cup garlic
wine vinegar
3 tsp caster (superfine) sugar

125 ml/4 fl oz/½ cup light soy
sauce
dash of chilli sauce
125 ml/4 fl oz/½ cup fish
stock
1 green (bell) pepper, seeded
and thinly sliced

1 large tomato, skinned,
seeded and cut into thin
strips
salt and pepper
sliced tomato, to garnish

1 Rinse the fish inside
and out and pat dry
with kitchen paper (paper
towels).

2 Make 3 diagonal slits
in the flesh on each
side of the fish. Season
with salt and pepper inside
and out.

3 Place the fish on a
heatproof plate and
scatter the spring onions
(scallions) and ginger over
the top. Cover and steam

for 10 minutes, or until the
fish is cooked through.

4 Place the vinegar,
sugar, soy sauce, chilli
sauce, fish stock, (bell)
pepper and tomato in a
saucepan and bring to the
boil, stirring occasionally.
Cook over a high heat
until the sauce has slightly
reduced and thickened.

5 Remove the fish from
the steamer and
transfer to a warm serving

dish. Pour the sauce over
the fish, garnish with
tomato slices and serve
immediately.

COOK'S TIP

*Use fillets of fish for this
recipe if preferred, and
reduce the cooking time
to 5–7 minutes.*

Szechuan White Fish

Serves 4

INGREDIENTS

350 g/12 oz white fish fillets
1 small egg, beaten
3 tbsp plain (all-purpose) flour
4 tbsp dry white wine
3 tbsp light soy sauce
vegetable oil, for frying
1 garlic clove, cut into slivers
1-cm/½-inch piece fresh root
   ginger, finely chopped

1 onion, finely chopped
1 celery stick, chopped
1 fresh red chilli, chopped
3 spring onions (scallions),
   chopped
1 tsp rice wine vinegar
½ tsp ground Szechuan
   pepper

175 ml/6 fl oz/¾ cup fish
   stock
1 tsp caster (superfine) sugar
1 tsp cornflour (cornstarch)
2 tsp water
chilli flowers and celery leaves,
   to garnish (optional)

1 Cut the fish into 4-cm/ 1½-inch cubes.

2 In a bowl, beat the egg, flour, wine and 1 tbsp of soy sauce to make a batter.

3 Dip the cubes of fish into the batter to coat.

4 Heat the oil in a preheated wok until it is almost smoking. Reduce the heat slightly and cook the fish, in batches, for 2–3 minutes, until golden. Drain on kitchen paper (paper towels) and set aside.

5 Pour all but 1 tbsp of oil from the wok and return to the heat. Add the garlic, ginger, onion, celery, chilli and spring onions (scallions) and stir-fry for 1–2 minutes.

6 Stir in the remaining soy sauce and the vinegar.

7 Add the Szechuan pepper, fish stock and sugar to the wok. Blend the cornflour (cornstarch) with the water to form a smooth paste and stir it into the stock. Bring to the boil and cook, stirring, for 1 minute, until the sauce thickens and clears.

8 Return the fish to the wok and cook for 1–2 minutes, until hot. Transfer to a serving dish.

Chicken With Cashew Nuts & Vegetables

Serves 4

INGREDIENTS

300 g/10¹/₂ oz boneless,
    skinless chicken breasts
1 tbsp cornflour (cornstarch)
1 tsp sesame oil
1 tbsp hoisin sauce
1 tsp light soy sauce
3 garlic cloves, crushed
2 tbsp vegetable oil

75 g/2³/₄ oz/³/₄ cup unsalted
    cashew nuts
25 g/1 oz mangetout (snow
    peas)
1 celery stick, sliced
1 onion, cut into 8 pieces
60 g/2 oz beansprouts

1 red (bell) pepper, seeded and
    diced

SAUCE:
2 tsp cornflour (cornstarch)
2 tbsp hoisin sauce
200 ml/7 fl oz/⁷/₈ cup chicken
    stock

1 Trim any fat from the chicken breasts and cut the meat into thin strips. Place the chicken in a large bowl. Sprinkle with the cornflour (cornstarch) and toss to coat the chicken strips in it, shaking off any excess. Mix together the sesame oil, hoisin sauce, soy sauce and 1 garlic clove. Pour this mixture over the chicken, turning to coat. Marinate for 20 minutes.

2 Heat half of the vegetable oil in a preheated wok. Add the cashew nuts and stir-fry for 1 minute, until browned. Add the mangetout (snow peas), celery, the remaining garlic, the onion, bean-sprouts and red (bell) pepper and cook, stirring occasionally, for 2–3 minutes. Remove the vegetables from the wok with a slotted spoon, set aside and keep warm.

3 Heat the remaining oil in the wok. Remove the chicken from the marinade and stir-fry for 3–4 minutes. Return the vegetables to the wok.

4 To make the sauce, mix the cornflour (cornstarch), hoisin sauce and chicken stock and pour into the wok. Bring to the boil, stirring until thickened and clear. Serve.

Spicy Peanut Chicken

Serves 4

INGREDIENTS
---

300 g/10½ oz skinless,
  boneless chicken breast
2 tbsp peanut oil
125 g/4½ oz/1 cup shelled
  peanuts
1 fresh red chilli, sliced
1 green (bell) pepper, seeded
  and cut into strips

1 tsp sesame oil
fried rice, to serve

SAUCE:
150 ml/¼ pint/⅔ cup chicken
  stock
1 tbsp Chinese rice wine or
  dry sherry

1 tbsp light soy sauce
1½ tsp light brown sugar
2 garlic cloves, crushed
1 tsp grated fresh root ginger
1 tsp rice wine vinegar

---

1 Trim any fat from the chicken and cut the meat into 2.5-cm/1-inch cubes. Set aside.

2 Heat the peanut oil in a preheated wok. Add the peanuts and stir-fry for 1 minute. Remove the peanuts with a slotted spoon and set aside.

3 Add the chicken to the wok and cook for 1–2 minutes. Stir in the chilli and (bell) pepper and cook

for 1 minute. Remove from the wok with a slotted spoon.

4 Put half of the peanuts in a food processor and process until almost smooth. Alternatively, place them in a plastic bag and crush with a rolling pin.

5 To make the sauce, add the chicken stock, Chinese rice wine or dry sherry, soy sauce, sugar, garlic, ginger and rice wine vinegar to the wok.

6 Heat the sauce without boiling and stir in the peanut purée, remaining peanuts, chicken, chilli and (bell) pepper. Sprinkle with the sesame oil, stir and cook for 1 minute. Serve hot.

COOK'S TIP

If necessary, process the peanuts with a little of the stock in step 4 to form a softer paste.

Bamboo Shoots with Spinach

Serves 4

INGREDIENTS

3 tbsp peanut oil
225 g/8 oz spinach, chopped
175 g/6 oz canned bamboo
    shoots, drained and rinsed
1 garlic clove, crushed

2 fresh red chillies, sliced
pinch of ground cinnamon
300 ml/½ pint/1¼ cups
    vegetable stock
pinch of sugar

pinch of salt
1 tbsp light soy sauce

1 Heat the peanut oil in a preheated wok.

2 Add the spinach and bamboo shoots to the wok and stir-fry for 1 minute.

3 Add the garlic, chilli and cinnamon to the mixture in the wok and stir-fry for a further 30 seconds.

4 Stir in the vegetable stock, sugar, salt and soy sauce, cover and cook over a medium heat for 5 minutes, or until the

vegetables are cooked through and the sauce has reduced. Transfer the bamboo shoots and spinach to a warm serving dish and serve.

COOK'S TIP

If there is too much liquid after 5 minutes cooking in step 4, blend a little cornflour (cornstarch) with double the quantity of cold water and stir into the sauce.

COOK'S TIP

Fresh bamboo shoots are rarely available in the West and, in any case, are extremely time-consuming to prepare. Canned bamboo shoots are quite satisfactory, as they are used to provide a crunchy texture, rather than for their flavour, which is fairly insipid.

Hot Spicy Lamb in Sauce

Serves 6–8

INGREDIENTS

175 ml/6 fl oz/³/₄ cup oil
1 kg/2 lb 4 oz lean leg of lamb,
    cut into large pieces
1 tbsp ground garam masala
5 medium onions, chopped
150 ml/5 fl oz/²/₃ cup yogurt
2 tbsp tomato purée (paste)
2 tsp fresh ginger root, finely
    chopped
2 tsp fresh garlic, crushed

1½ tsp salt
2 tsp chilli powder
1 tbsp ground coriander
2 tsp ground nutmeg
900 ml/1½ pints/3³/₄ cups
    water
1 tbsp ground fennel seeds
1 tbsp paprika
1 tbsp bhoonay chanay or
    gram flour

3 bay leaves
1 tbsp plain (all-purpose) flour
naan breads or paratas, to
    serve

TO GARNISH:
2–3 green chillies, chopped
fresh coriander (cilantro)
    leaves, chopped

1 Heat the oil in a pan and add the meat and half of the garam masala. Stir-fry the mixture for 7–10 minutes until the meat is well coated. Using a perforated spoon, remove the meat and set aside.

2 Fry the onions in the pan until golden. Then return the meat to the pan, reduce the heat and simmer, stirring regularly.

3 In a separate bowl, mix the yogurt and tomato purée (paste), ginger, garlic, salt, chilli powder, ground coriander, nutmeg and the rest of the garam masala. Pour this mixture over the meat and stir-fry, mixing the spices well into the meat, for 5–7 minutes.

4 Add half of the water, then the fennel, paprika and *bhoonay chanay* or gram flour. Add the remaining water and bay leaves, lower heat, cover and cook for 1 hour.

5 Mix the flour in 2 tbsp of warm water and pour over the curry. Garnish with the chillies and the coriander (cilantro); cook until the meat is tender and the sauce thickens. Serve with Naan or Paratas.

Cubed Lamb Kebabs (Kabobs)

Serves 6–8

INGREDIENTS

1 kg/2 lb 4 oz lean lamb, boned and cubed
1 tsp meat tenderizer
1½ tsp fresh ginger root, finely chopped
1½ tsp fresh garlic, crushed
1 tsp chilli powder

½ tsp turmeric
½ tsp salt
2 tbsp water
8 tomatoes, cut in half
8 small pickling onions
10 mushrooms

1 green (bell) pepper, cut into large pieces
1 red (bell) pepper, cut into large pieces
2 tbsp oil
2 lemons, cut into quarters, to garnish

1 Wash the cubed lamb and place it in a clean dish. Apply the tenderizer to the meat, using your hands. Then set the dish aside for about 3 hours at room temperature.

2 Mix together the ginger, garlic, chilli powder, turmeric and salt in a bowl. Add the water and mix with the spices to form a paste. Add the cubed meat and mix until it is well coated with the spice mixture.

3 Arrange the meat cubes on skewers, alternating with the tomatoes, pickling onions, mushrooms and (bell) peppers. Brush the meat and vegetables with the oil.

4 Grill (broil) the kebabs (kabobs) under a pre-heated grill (broiler) for 25–30 minutes or until the meat is cooked through. When cooked, remove the kebabs (kabobs) from the grill (broiler) and transfer to a serving plate. Arrange

lemon wedges on the side and serve immediately with boiled rice.

COOK'S TIP

If using wooden skewers, soak them in cold water for 20 minutes before they are used to prevent them from burning during cooking.

Beef Khorma with Almonds

Serves 6

INGREDIENTS

300 ml/½ pint/1¼ cups oil
3 medium onions, finely
    chopped
1 kg/2 lb 4 oz lean beef, cubed
1½ tsp garam masala
1½ tsp ground coriander
1½ tsp fresh ginger root,
    finely chopped

1½ tsp fresh garlic, crushed
1 tsp salt
150 ml/5 fl oz/⅔ cup natural
    yogurt
2 cloves
3 green cardamoms
4 black peppercorns
600 ml/1 pint/2½ cups water

TO GARNISH:
6 almonds, soaked, peeled and
    chopped
2 green chillies, chopped
a few fresh coriander
    (cilantro) leaves

1 Heat the oil in a saucepan. Add the onions and stir-fry until golden brown.

2 Add the meat to the onions in the pan and stir-fry for about 5 minutes. Remove the pan from the heat.

3 Mix the garam masala, ground coriander, ginger, garlic, salt and yogurt in a bowl. Gradually add the meat to the yogurt and spice mixture and mix to coat the meat on all sides. Place in the saucepan, return to the heat, and stir-fry for 5–7 minutes, or until the mixture is nearly brown in colour.

4 Add the cloves, green cardamoms and black peppercorns. Add the water, lower the heat, cover and leave to simmer for about 45–60 minutes. If the water has completely evaporated but the meat is still not tender enough, add another 300 ml/½ pint/1½ cups water and cook for a further 10–15 minutes, stirring occasionally.

5 Just before serving, garnish with chopped almonds, green chillies and the fresh coriander (cilantro) leaves. Serve with Chapatis.

Chicken Jalfrezi

Serves 4

INGREDIENTS

1 tsp mustard oil
3 tbsp vegetable oil
1 large onion, chopped finely
3 garlic cloves, crushed
1 tbsp tomato purée (paste)
2 tomatoes, peeled and
 chopped
1 tsp ground turmeric

$\frac{1}{2}$ tsp cumin seeds, ground
$\frac{1}{2}$ tsp coriander seeds, ground
$\frac{1}{2}$ tsp chilli powder
$\frac{1}{2}$ tsp garam masala
1 tsp red wine vinegar
1 small red (bell) pepper,
 chopped

125 g/4 oz/1 cup frozen broad
 (fava) beans
500 g/1 lb cooked chicken
 breasts, cut into bite-sized
 pieces
salt
fresh coriander (cilantro)
 sprigs, to garnish

1 Heat the mustard oil in a large, frying pan (skillet) set over a high heat for about 1 minute until it begins to smoke. Add the vegetable oil, reduce the heat and then add the onion and the garlic. Fry the garlic and onion until they are golden.

2 Add the tomato purée (paste), chopped tomatoes, ground turmeric, cumin and coriander seeds, chilli powder, garam masala and red wine vinegar to the frying pan (skillet). Stir the mixture until fragrant.

3 Add the red (bell) pepper and broad (fava) beans and stir for 2 minutes until the (bell) pepper is softened. Stir in the chicken, and salt to taste. Leave the curry to simmer gently for 6–8 minutes until the chicken is heated through and the beans are tender.

4 Serve garnished with coriander (cilantro).

COOK'S TIP

This dish is an ideal way of making use of leftover poultry – turkey, duck or quail. Any variety of beans works well, but vegetables are just as useful, especially root vegetables, courgettes (zucchini), potatoes or broccoli. Leafy vegetables will not be so successful.

Prawns (Shrimp) with Tomatoes

Serves 4–6

INGREDIENTS

3 medium onions
1 green (bell) pepper
1 tsp fresh ginger root, finely
   chopped
1 tsp fresh garlic, crushed

1 tsp salt
1 tsp chilli powder
2 tbsp lemon juice
350 g/12 oz frozen prawns
   (shrimp)

3 tbsp oil
400 g/14 oz can tomatoes
fresh coriander (cilantro)
   leaves, to garnish

1 Using a sharp knife, slice the onions and the green (bell) pepper.

2 Place the ginger, garlic, salt and chilli powder in a small bowl and mix. Add the lemon juice and mix to form a paste.

3 Place the prawns (shrimp) in a bowl of cold water and set aside to defrost. Drain thoroughly.

4 Heat the oil in a medium-sized saucepan. Add the onions and fry until golden brown.

5 Add the spice paste to the onions, reduce the heat to low and cook, stirring and mixing well, for about 3 minutes.

6 Add the tomatoes, tomato juice and the green (bell) pepper, and cook for 5–7 minutes, stirring occasionally.

7 Add the defrosted prawns (shrimp) to the pan and cook the mixture for about 10 minutes, stirring occasionally. Garnish with fresh coriander (cilantro) leaves

and serve hot with plain boiled rice and a crisp green salad.

COOK'S TIP

Fresh ginger root looks rather like a knobbly potato. The skin should be peeled, then the flesh either grated, finely chopped or sliced. Ginger is also available ground: this can be used as a substitute for fresh root ginger, but the fresh root is far superior.

Green Bean & Potato Curry

Serves 4

INGREDIENTS
---

300 ml/¹/₂ pint/1¹/₄ cups oil
1 tsp white cumin seeds
1 tsp mustard and onion seeds
4 dried red chillies
3 fresh tomatoes, sliced
1 tsp salt

1 tsp fresh ginger root, finely
   chopped
1 tsp fresh garlic, crushed
1 tsp chilli powder
200 g/7 oz green cut beans
2 medium potatoes, peeled
   and diced

300 ml/¹/₂ pint/1¹/₄ cups water
fresh coriander (cilantro)
   leaves, chopped
2 green chillies, finely chopped

---

1 Heat the oil in a large, heavy-based saucepan.

2 Add the white cumin seeds, mustard and onion seeds and dried red chillies to the saucepan, stirring well.

3 Add the tomato slices to the saucepan and stir-fry the mixture for 3–5 minutes.

4 Mix together the salt, ginger, garlic and chilli powder and spoon into the pan. Blend the whole mixture together.

5 Add the green beans and potatoes to the pan and stir-fry for about 5 minutes.

6 Add the water to the pan, reduce the heat and leave to simmer for 10–15 minutes, stirring occasionally.

7 Garnish the green bean and potato curry with chopped coriander (cilantro) leaves and green chillies and serve hot with cooked rice.

COOK'S TIP

Mustard seeds are often fried in oil or ghee to bring out their flavour before being combined with other ingredients.

Spinach & Cheese Curry

Serves 4

INGREDIENTS

300 ml/¹/₂ pint/1¹/₄ cups oil
200 g/7 oz panir, cubed (see
    Cook's Tip)

3 tomatoes, sliced
1 tsp ground cumin
1¹/₂ tsp ground chilli powder

1 tsp salt
400 g/14 oz spinach
3 green chillies

1 Heat the oil in a large frying pan (skillet). Add the cubed panir and fry, stirring occasionally, until golden brown.

2 Remove the panir from the frying pan (skillet) with a perforated spoon and leave to drain on kitchen paper.

3 Add the tomatoes to the remaining oil in the pan and stir-fry, breaking up the tomatoes, for 5 minutes.

4 Add the ground cumin, chilli powder and salt and mix well.

5 Add the spinach to the pan and stir-fry over a low heat for 7–10 minutes.

6 Add the green chillies and the panir and cook, stirring, for a further 2 minutes.

7 Transfer the curry to serving plates and serve hot with pooris or plain boiled rice.

VARIATION

You could used frozen spinach in this recipe. It should be thawed and squeezed dry before using.

COOK'S TIP

To make panir, boil 1 litre/ 1³/₄ pints/4¹/₂ cups milk slowly over a low heat, then add 2 tbsp lemon juice, stirring continuously and gently until the milk thickens and begins to curdle. Strain the curdled milk through a sieve. Set aside under a heavy weight for about 1¹/₂–2 hours to press to a flat shape about 1 cm/¹/₂ inch thick. Once set, the panir can be cut, like cheese, into whatever shape is required.

Chickpea (Garbanzo Bean) Curry

Serves 4

INGREDIENTS

6 tbsp oil
2 medium onions, sliced
1 tsp fresh ginger root, finely
   chopped
1 tsp ground cumin

1 tsp ground coriander
1 tsp fresh garlic, crushed
1 tsp chilli powder
2 fresh green chillies
fresh coriander (cilantro)
   leaves

150 ml/^{1}/$_4$ pint/^{2}/$_3$ cup water
1 large potato
400 g/14 oz can chickpeas
   (garbanzo beans), drained
1 tbsp lemon juice

1 Heat the oil in a large saucepan.

2 Add the sliced onions to the pan and fry, stirring occasionally, until golden brown.

3 Reduce the heat, then add the ginger, ground cumin, ground coriander, garlic, chilli powder, chopped fresh green chillies and fresh coriander (cilantro) leaves to the saucepan, stirring the ingredients constantly for about 2 minutes.

4 Add the water to the mixture in the pan and stir to mix.

5 Using a sharp knife, cut the potato into small dice.

6 Add the potatoes and the drained chickpeas (garbanzo beans) to the mixture in the pan, cover and leave to simmer, stirring occasionally, for 5–7 minutes.

7 Sprinkle the lemon juice over the curry.

8 Transfer the chickpea (garbanzo bean) curry to serving dishes. Serve the curry hot with chapati, if you wish.

COOK'S TIP

Using canned chickpeas (garbanzo beans) saves time, but you can use dried chickpeas (garbanzo beans) if you prefer. Soak them overnight, then boil them for 15–20 minutes or until soft.

Lemon Dhaal

Serves 4

INGREDIENTS
---

100 g/3¹/₂ oz/¹/₂ cup
  masoor dhaal
1 tsp fresh ginger root, finely
  chopped
1 tsp fresh garlic, crushed
1 tsp chilli powder
¹/₂ tsp turmeric

425 ml/³/₄ pint/2 cups water
1 tsp salt
3 tbsp lemon juice
2 green chillies
fresh coriander (cilantro)
  leaves

BAGHAAR:
150 ml/¹/₄ pint/²/₃ cup oil
4 whole garlic cloves
6 dried red chillies
1 tsp white cumin seeds

---

1 Rinse the *masoor dhaal* and place in a large saucepan.

2 Add the ginger, garlic, chilli powder and turmeric to the *dhaal*. Stir in 300 ml/¹/₂ pint/1¹/₄ cups of the water and bring to a boil over a medium heat with the lid left slightly ajar until the *dhaal* is soft enough to be mashed.

3 Mash the *dhaal*. Add the salt, lemon juice and 150 ml/¹/₄ pint/²/₃ cup of the water, stir and mix well. It should be of a fairly smooth consistency.

4 Add the green chillies and fresh coriander (cilantro) leaves to the *dhaal* and set aside.

5 To make the *baghaar*, heat the oil in a pan. Add the garlic, red chillies and white cumin seeds and fry for about 1 minute. Turn off the heat, then when the heat has been reduced pour the *baghaar* over the *dhaal*. If the *dhaal* is too runny cook over a medium heat with the lid off for 3–5 minutes.

6 Transfer to a serving dish and serve hot.

COOK'S TIP

This dish is a good accompaniment to Beef Khorma with Almonds (see page 42).

Brown Rice with Fruit & Nuts

Serves 4–6

INGREDIENTS

4 tbsp vegetable ghee or oil
1 large onion, chopped
2 garlic cloves, crushed
2.5 cm/1 inch ginger root,
  chopped finely
1 tsp chilli powder
1 tsp cumin seeds
1 tbsp mild or medium curry
  powder or paste

300 g/10 oz/1½ cups brown
  rice
850 ml/1½ pints/3½ cups
  boiling vegetable stock
400 g/14 oz can chopped
  tomatoes
175 g/6 oz ready-soaked dried
  apricots or peaches, cut
  into slivers

1 red (bell) pepper, cored,
  seeded and diced
90 g/3 oz frozen peas
1–2 small, slightly green
  bananas
60–90 g/2–3oz/⅓–½ cup
  toasted mixed nuts
salt and pepper

1 Heat the ghee or oil in a large saucepan, add the onion and fry gently for 3 minutes.

2 Stir in the garlic, ginger, chilli powder, cumin seeds, curry powder or paste and rice. Cook gently for 2 minutes, stirring, until the rice is coated in the spiced oil.

3 Pour in the boiling stock, stirring to mix.

Add the tomatoes and season with salt and pepper. Bring to the boil, then reduce the heat, cover and leave to simmer gently for 40 minutes or until the rice is almost cooked and most of the liquid is absorbed.

4 Add the apricots or peaches, red (bell) pepper and peas to the rice mixture in the pan. Cover and continue cooking for 10 minutes.

5 Remove the pan from the heat and leave to stand for 5 minutes without uncovering.

6 Peel and slice the bananas. Uncover the rice mixture and toss with a fork to mix. Add the toasted nuts and sliced banana and toss lightly.

7 Transfer the rice dish to a serving platter and serve hot.

Stir-Fried Ginger Chicken

Serves 4

> **INGREDIENTS**

2 tbsp sunflower oil
1 onion, sliced
175 g/6 oz carrots, cut into thin
　sticks
1 clove garlic, crushed
350 g/12 oz boneless skinless
　chicken breasts

2 tbsp fresh ginger, peeled and
　grated
1 tsp ground ginger
4 tbsp sweet sherry
1 tbsp tomato purée
1 tbsp demerara sugar

100 ml/3$\frac{1}{2}$ fl oz/$\frac{1}{2}$ cup orange
　juice
1 tsp cornflour (cornstarch)
1 orange, peeled and segmented
fresh snipped chives, to garnish

1 Heat the oil in a large preheated wok. Add the onion, carrots and garlic and stir-fry over a high heat for 3 minutes or until the vegetables begin to soften.

2 Using a sharp knife, slice the chicken into thin strips. Add the chicken to the wok together with the fresh ginger and ground ginger. Stir-fry for a further 10 minutes, or until the chicken is well cooked through and golden in colour.

3 Mix together the sherry, tomato purée, sugar, orange juice and cornflour (cornstarch) in a bowl. Stir the mixture into the wok and heat through until the mixture bubbles and the juices start to thicken.

4 Add the orange segments and carefully toss to mix.

5 Transfer the stir-fried chicken to warm serving bowls and garnish with freshly snipped chives. Serve immediately.

COOK'S TIP

Make sure that you do not continue cooking the dish once the orange segments have been added in step 4, otherwise they will break up.

Chicken, (Bell) Pepper & Orange Stir-Fry

Serves 4

INGREDIENTS

3 tbsp sunflower oil

350 g/12 oz boneless chicken thighs, skinned and cut into thin strips

1 onion, sliced

1 clove garlic, crushed

1 red (bell) pepper, deseeded and sliced

75 g/2³⁄₄ oz/1¹⁄₄ cups mangetout (snow peas)

4 tbsp light soy sauce

4 tbsp sherry

1 tbsp tomato purée

finely grated rind and juice of 1 orange

1 tsp cornflour (cornstarch)

2 oranges

100 g/3¹⁄₂ oz/1 cup beansprouts

cooked rice or noodles, to serve

1 Heat the sunflower oil in a large preheated wok.

2 Add the strips of chicken to the wok and stir-fry for 2–3 minutes or until sealed on all sides.

3 Add the sliced onion, garlic, (bell) pepper and mangetout (snow peas) to the wok. Stir-fry the mixture for a further 5 minutes, or until the vegetables are just becoming tender and the chicken is completely cooked through.

4 Mix together the soy sauce, sherry, tomato purée, orange rind and juice and the cornflour (cornstarch) in a measuring jug.

5 Add the mixture to the wok and cook, stirring, until the juices start to thicken.

6 Using a sharp knife, peel and segment the oranges.

7 Add the orange segments and bean-sprouts to the mixture in the wok and heat through for a further 2 minutes.

8 Transfer the stir-fry to serving plates and serve at once with cooked rice or noodles.

COOK'S TIP

Beansprouts are sprouting mung beans and are a regular ingredient in Chinese cooking. They require very little cooking and may even be eaten raw, if wished.

Hoisin Duck with Leek & Stir-Fried Cabbage

Serves 4

INGREDIENTS

4 duck breasts	225 g/8 oz leeks, sliced	1 tsp toasted sesame seeds, to
350 g/12 oz green cabbage, thinly shredded	finely grated zest of 1 orange	serve
	6 tbsp oyster sauce	

1 Heat a large wok and dry-fry the duck breasts, with the skin on, for 5 minutes on each side (you may need to do this in 2 batches).

2 Remove the duck breasts from the wok and transfer to a clean board. Using a sharp knife, cut the duck breasts into thin slices.

3 Remove all but 1 tablespoon of the fat from the duck left in the wok; discard the rest.

4 Using a sharp knife, thinly shred the green cabbage.

5 Add the leeks, green cabbage and orange zest to the wok and stir-fry for 5 minutes, or until the vegetables have softened.

6 Return the duck to the wok and heat through for 2–3 minutes.

7 Drizzle the oyster sauce over the top of the duck, toss well to combine and then heat through.

8 Scatter with toasted sesame seeds and serve hot.

VARIATION

Use Chinese leaves for a lighter, sweeter flavour instead of the green cabbage, if you prefer.

Pork Fillet Stir-Fry with Crunchy Satay Sauce

Serves 4

INGREDIENTS

150 g/5½ oz carrots	1 yellow (bell) pepper, deseeded	SATAY SAUCE:
2 tbsp sunflower oil	and sliced	6 tbsp crunchy peanut butter
350 g/12 oz pork neck fillet, thinly	150 g/5½ oz/2⅓ cups mangetout	6 tbsp coconut milk
sliced	(snow peas)	1 tsp chilli flakes
1 onion, sliced	75 g/3 oz/1½ cups fine asparagus	1 clove garlic, crushed
2 cloves garlic, crushed	chopped salted peanuts, to serve	1 tsp tomato purée

1 Using a sharp knife, slice the carrots into thin sticks.

2 Heat the oil in a large wok. Add the pork, onion and garlic and stir-fry for 5 minutes or until the lamb is cooked through.

3 Add the carrots, (bell) pepper, mangetout (snow peas) and asparagus to the wok and stir-fry for 5 minutes.

4 To make the satay sauce, place the peanut butter, coconut milk, chilli flakes, garlic and tomato purée in a small pan and heat gently, stirring, until well combined.

5 Transfer the stir-fry to warm serving plates. Spoon the satay sauce over the stir-fry and scatter with chopped peanuts. Serve immediately.

COOK'S TIP

Cook the sauce just before serving as it tends to thicken very quickly and will not be spoonable if you cook it too far in advance.

Spicy Pork Balls

Serves 4

INGREDIENTS

450 g/1 lb pork mince
2 shallots, finely chopped
2 cloves garlic, crushed
1 tsp cumin seeds
½ tsp chilli powder

25 g/1 oz/½ cup wholemeal
 (whole wheat) breadcrumbs
1 egg, beaten
2 tbsp sunflower oil
400 g/14 oz can chopped
 tomatoes, flavoured with chilli

2 tbsp soy sauce
200 g/7 oz can water chestnuts,
 drained
3 tbsp chopped fresh coriander
 (cilantro)

---

1 Place the pork mince in a large mixing bowl. Add the shallots, garlic, cumin seeds, chilli powder, breadcrumbs and beaten egg and mix together well.

2 Take small pieces of the mixture and form into balls between the palms of your hands.

3 Heat the sunflower oil in a large preheated wok. Add the pork balls to the wok and stir-fry, in batches, over a high heat for about 5 minutes or until sealed on all sides.

4 Add the tomatoes, soy sauce and water chestnuts and bring to the boil. Return the pork balls to the wok, reduce the heat and leave to simmer for 15 minutes.

5 Scatter with chopped fresh coriander (cilantro) and serve hot.

COOK'S TIP

Add a few teaspoons of chilli sauce to a tin of chopped tomatoes, if you can't find the flavoured variety.

COOK'S TIP

Coriander (cilantro) is also known as Chinese parsley, but has a much stronger flavour and should be used with care. Parsley is not a viable alternative; use basil if coriander (cilantro) is not available.

Spring Onion (Scallion) & Lamb Stir-Fry with Oyster Sauce

Serves 4

INGREDIENTS

450 g/1 lb lamb leg steaks	2 cloves garlic, crushed	175 g/6 oz Chinese leaves
1 tsp ground Szechuan peppercorns	8 spring onions (scallions), sliced	prawn (shrimp) crackers, to serve
1 tbsp groundnut oil	2 tbsp dark soy sauce	
	6 tbsp oyster sauce	

1 Using a sharp knife, remove any excess fat from the lamb. Slice the lamb thinly.

2 Sprinkle the ground Szechuan peppercorns over the meat and toss together until well combined.

3 Heat the oil in a preheated wok. Add the lamb and stir-fry for 5 minutes.

4 Mix the garlic, spring onions (scallions) and soy sauce, add to the wok and stir-fry for 2 minutes.

5 Add the oyster sauce and Chinese leaves and stir-fry for a further 2 minutes, or until the leaves have wilted and the juices are bubbling.

6 Transfer the stir-fry to warm serving bowls and serve hot.

COOK'S TIP

Oyster sauce is made from oysters which are cooked in brine and soy sauce. Sold in bottles, it will keep in the refrigerator for months.

COOK'S TIP

Prawn (shrimp) crackers consist of compressed slivers of prawn (shrimp) and flour paste. They expand when deep-fried.

Teriyaki Stir-Fried Salmon with Crispy Leeks

Serves 4

INGREDIENTS

450 g/1 lb salmon fillet, skinned	1 tsp rice wine vinegar	4 tbsp corn oil
2 tbsp sweet soy sauce	1 tbsp demerara sugar	450 g/1 lb leeks, thinly shredded
2 tbsp tomato ketchup	1 clove garlic, crushed	finely chopped red chillies, to garnish

1 Using a sharp knife, cut the salmon into slices. Place the slices of salmon in a shallow non-metallic dish.

2 Mix together the soy sauce, tomato ketchup, rice wine vinegar, sugar and garlic.

3 Pour the mixture over the salmon, toss well and leave to marinate for about 30 minutes.

4 Meanwhile, heat 3 tablespoons of the corn oil in a large preheated wok.

5 Add the leeks to the wok and stir-fry over a medium high heat for about 10 minutes, or until the leeks become crispy and tender.

6 Using a slotted spoon, carefully remove the leeks from the wok and transfer to warmed serving plates.

7 Add the remaining oil to the wok. Add the salmon and the marinade to the wok and cook for 2 minutes. Spoon over the leeks, garnish and serve immediately.

VARIATION

You can use a fillet of beef instead of the salmon, if you prefer.

Stir-Fried Gingered Monkfish

Serves 4

INGREDIENTS

450 g/1 lb monkfish	1 tbsp corn oil	3 spring onions (scallions), sliced
1 tbsp freshly grated root ginger	100 g/3½ oz/1 cup fine asparagus	1 tsp sesame oil
2 tbsp sweet chilli sauce		

1 Using a sharp knife, slice the monkfish into thin flat rounds.

2 Mix the ginger with the chilli sauce in a small bowl.

3 Brush the ginger and chilli sauce mixture over the monkfish pieces.

4 Heat the corn oil in a large preheated wok.

5 Add the monkfish, asparagus and spring onions (scallions) to the wok and stir-fry for about 5 minutes.

6 Remove the wok from the heat, drizzle the sesame oil over the stir-fry and toss well to combine.

7 Transfer to warm serving plates and serve immediately.

VARIATION

Monkfish is quite expensive, but it is well worth using it as it has a wonderful flavour and texture. At a push you could use cubes of chunky cod fillet instead.

COOK'S TIP

Some recipes specify to grate ginger before it is cooked with other ingredients. To do this, just peel the flesh and rub it at a 45° angle up and down on the fine section of a metal grater, or use a special wooden or ceramic ginger grater.

Japanese Noodles with Spicy Vegetables

Serves 4

INGREDIENTS

450 g/1 lb fresh Japanese noodles
1 tbsp sesame oil
1 tbsp sesame seeds
1 tbsp sunflower oil
1 red onion, sliced

100 g/3½ oz mangetout,
  (snow peas)
175 g/6 oz carrots, thinly sliced
350 g/12 oz white cabbage,
  shredded

3 tbsp sweet chilli sauce
2 spring onions (scallions), sliced,
  to garnish

1 Bring a large saucepan of water to the boil. Add the Japanese noodles to the pan and cook for 2–3 minutes. Drain the noodles thoroughly.

2 Toss the noodles with the sesame oil and sesame seeds.

3 Heat the sunflower oil in a large preheated wok.

4 Add the onion slices, mangetout (snow peas), carrot slices and shredded cabbage to the wok and stir-fry for about 5 minutes.

5 Add the sweet chilli sauce to the wok and cook, stirring occasionally, for a further 2 minutes.

6 Add the sesame noodles to the wok, toss well to combine and heat through for a further 2–3 minutes. (You may wish to serve the noodles separately, so transfer them to the serving bowls.)

7 Transfer the Japanese noodles and spicy vegetables to warm serving bowls and garnish with sliced spring onions (scallions). Serve.

COOK'S TIP

If fresh Japanese noodles are difficult to get hold of, use dried rice noodles or thin egg noodles instead.

Naan Bread

Makes 6-8

INGREDIENTS

1 tsp sugar
1 tsp fresh yeast
150 ml/¹/₄ pint/²/₃ cup warm
   water

200 g/7 oz/1¹/₂ cups plain
   (all-purpose) flour
1 tbsp ghee

1 tsp salt
50 g/1³/₄ oz/6 tbsp unsalted
   butter
1 tsp poppy seeds

1 Put the sugar and yeast in a small bowl or jug with the warm water and mix well until the yeast has dissolved. Set aside for about 10 minutes or until the mixture is frothy.

2 Place the flour in a large mixing bowl. Make a well in the middle of the flour, add the ghee and salt and pour in the yeast mixture. Mix well to form a dough, using your hands and adding more water if required.

3 Turn the dough out on to a floured surface

and knead for 5 minutes or until smooth.

4 Return the dough to the bowl, cover and leave to rise in a warm place for 1¹/₂ hours or until doubled in size.

5 Turn the dough out on to a floured surface and knead for a further 2 minutes. Break off small balls with your hand and pat them into rounds about 12 cm/5 inches in diameter and 1 cm/¹/₂ inch thick.

6 Place the dough rounds on to a greased

sheet of foil and grill (broil) under a very hot pre-heated grill (broiler) for 7–10 minutes, turning twice and brushing with the butter and sprinkling with the poppy seeds.

7 Serve warm immediately, or keep wrapped in foil until required.

Indian Pakoras

Serves 4

INGREDIENTS

6 tbsp gram flour
1/2 tsp salt
1 tsp chilli powder
1 tsp baking powder
1 1/2 tsp white cumin seeds

1 tsp pomegranate seeds
300 ml/1/2 pint/1 1/4 cups water
fresh coriander (cilantro)
  leaves, finely chopped

vegetables of your choice:
  cauliflower, cut into small
  florets, onions, cut into
  rings, potatoes, sliced,
  aubergines (eggplants),
  sliced, or fresh spinach
  leaves)
oil, for deep-frying

1 Sift the gram flour into a large mixing bowl.

2 Add the salt, chilli powder, baking powder, cumin and pomegranate seeds and blend together well.

3 Pour in the water and beat well to form a smooth batter.

4 Add the coriander (cilantro) and mix. Set the batter aside.

5 Dip the prepared vegetables of your choice into the batter, carefully shaking off any of the excess batter.

6 Heat the oil in a large heavy-based pan. Place the battered vegetables of your choice in the oil and deep-fry, in batches, turning once.

7 Repeat this process until all of the batter has been used up.

8 Transfer the battered vegetables to kitchen paper and drain. Serve immediately.

COOK'S TIP

When deep-frying, it is important to use oil at the correct temperature. If it is too hot, the outside of the food will burn before the inside is cooked. If too cool, the food will be sodden with oil before a batter forms.

This is a Parragon Book
First published in 2000

Parragon
Queen Street House
4 Queen Street
Bath BA1 1HE, UK

ISBN: 0-75253-615-X

Copyright © Parragon 2000

Printed in China

Note

Cup measurements in this book are for American cups. Tablespoons are assumed to be
15 ml. Unless otherwise stated, milk is assumed to be full fat, eggs are medium and
pepper is freshly ground black pepper.